Highlights

The Highlights Book of
Things to
DRAW

HIGHLIGHTS PRESS
HONESDALE, PENNSYLVANIA

CONTENTS

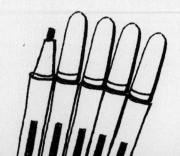

HOW TO USE THIS BOOK

There are no rules on how to use this book. You can open it to any page you'd like—and come back to any other page that interests you. If you know you'd like to draw animals, you can open up to the chapter called "Go Wild!" Or if you feel like drawing a cool fantasy scene, you can go to "Adventure." If you want to practice different drawing styles, you can flip to "Practice Drawing." And if you are short on time, try our "6 Quick Challenges" at the beginning of every chapter. The great thing is you don't have to worry about what to draw. We've given you lots of ideas to try out.

And if you're having trouble deciding what to draw, just keep doodling. Remember that art is about expressing yourself and creating something new, but it's also about having fun. If a drawing isn't coming out the way you wanted it to, that's okay! Sometimes an artist's "mistakes" can lead to inspiration or even great masterpieces.

USING RECYCLED AND ECO-FRIENDLY MATERIALS

There are many projects in this book that you can make with materials that are already in your home. We encourage you to use recycled, scrap, or environmentally friendly products as much as possible in activities that require paper, cardboard, plastic bottles, paper bags, plastic containers, and similar items. We hope that this book will inspire you to consider what goes into the things you make and use, and how those things may impact the planet.

SAFETY FIRST!

Some activities ask you to work with things that are hot and/or sharp. It is important to learn how to use dangerous tools and equipment safely. We have noted when it is necessary to have a grown-up help you. We also tell you when a grown-up will need to use a tool or piece of equipment for you.

Draw an animal you like using your dominant hand (the hand you usually use to write). Then draw it again using your other hand.

Quick Challenges
PRACTICE DRAWING

6

Pick a letter of the alphabet. Draw five things that start with that letter.

Find or print out a photograph or drawing you really like, and then try tracing it.

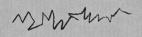

Fill up this page with doodles.

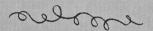

Have a friend start a drawing, and then finish the other half.

Try drawing the same object in different types of lighting.
How do the shadows change?

Patterns

A pattern is a design that repeats itself. Patterns can be used as decoration, and they can also be found in nature. Here are some fun patterns you can draw in the space below. Can you think of any others?

 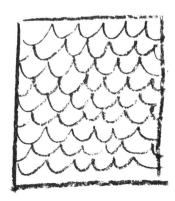 

Whoosh! Give these hot-air balloons some fun patterns.

Tip! What patterns can you find on animals and plants? Try using some of the patterns you see outside in your art.

Art Styles

Experimenting with different styles can help you grow as an artist . . . and can be really fun! Pick one subject that you want to draw (like an object, a person, or a nature scene), and then try drawing it in these three different styles. Which one is your favorite?

Comic

Draw how your object might look in a classic comic.

Realistic

Try to draw your object as realistically as possible.

Lots of Dots

Draw your object using just small dots of different colors to make up the larger picture.

In Style

The way that an artist chooses to paint or draw is known as their style. Some artists have become well-known for their unique styles. Some styles have also become famous and have been used by lots of artists. When one style becomes popular with many artists at the same time, it is called an art movement.

Shapes

Shapes are everywhere you look. Thinking about what shapes make up an object is a great way to practice drawing. Try drawing a farmyard with some animals using shapes. Start by drawing the horse shown here or create some from your imagination.

1.

2.

3.

4.

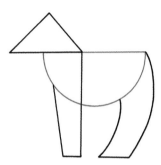

5.

Connect the Dots

Ahoy! Connecting the dots can help you practice your drawing skills. Count by sixes and connect the dots below to find out what new undersea voyage awaits. Once you've revealed the image, try drawing your own version on the next page.

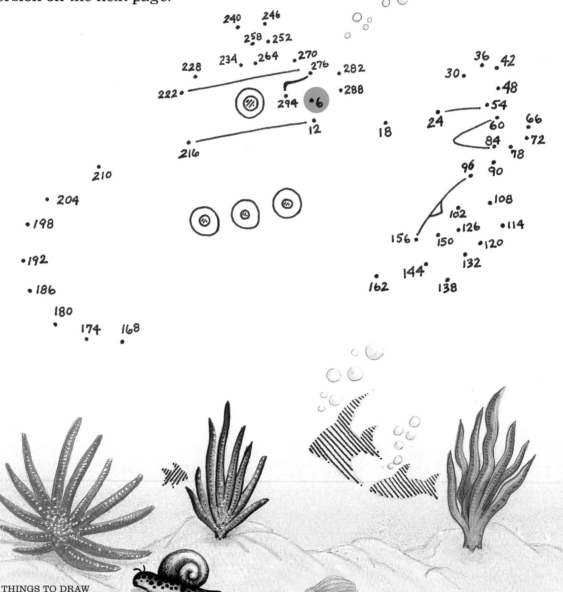

Upside Down

When you look at an object you know well, your brain is often too familiar with it to really "see" all the little details. It may sound strange, but looking at the object upside down can trick your mind into seeing all the shapes, curves, and spaces that make up the object. Find a simple object or photograph of something you want to draw. First, draw your object below.

Next, flip the object or photograph upside
down and draw it on this page! Which
version do you like better?

**More
Ideas!**
Try drawing a very
small version of your
object and then a
very large version.
How does changing
the size help you
notice new
details?

Upcycled Art

Take your art to the next level, and make a statement about cleaning up Earth by adding recycled materials to your masterpiece. Try these tips below or come up with your own.

Mixed Media
Glue or tape recycled and reused items directly onto your drawing. Try making a nature scene using sticks as tree trunks, a bottle cap as the sun, and more.

Cool Collage
Make a work of art by cutting out images from old magazines and newspapers and gluing them together to create new scenes.

Fantastic Frames
Make a fancy frame for your drawing out of recycled straws, foil lids, ribbons, or other reused materials.

Creative Canvas
Try drawing on something unexpected, like a rinsed milk carton or a grocery bag.

Drawing Games

Make new crayons out of broken crayon pieces.

You Need

- Crayon pieces
- Knife
- Muffin or cupcake tin
- Foil
- Pot holders or oven mitts

1. Have an adult help you with anything hot. Preheat your oven to 250°F. Line each cup with foil to keep the wax from sticking.

2. Ask an adult to help you chop the crayons into tiny pieces about half an inch long (or smaller).

3. Place the crayon pieces into each cup in the muffin tin to a height of about half an inch. Mix and match the colors however you want.

4. Have an adult help you put the muffin tin into the oven.

5. Bake for about 20 minutes or until the wax has melted.

6. Have an adult help you take the tin out of the oven. Allow your new crayons to cool completely before removing them from the tin. How do you like the shape of your crayons?

7. Make a masterpiece!

Tip!
Try using different baking molds to create cool new crayons with fun shapes.

Texture

Adding texture—the way an object's surface looks and feels—
to a drawing can make it seem more lifelike. Practice drawing
texture by giving these people and animals some fancy hairdos.

Abstract Art

Not all art shows an object, a person, or a scene. Some artists use colors, lines, forms, textures, or shapes to represent emotions, places, animals, and people. This is called abstract art. Try creating multiple abstract art pieces here. Pick something you want to draw, and then depict it using only shapes or colors—or both!

ART STYLES

There is no right or wrong way to make abstract art. Here are some famous styles to get you started:

Shapes

Some artists use only shapes and color to represent animals, places, and people. Others arrange dots and lines to make the viewers feel different emotions.

Paint Splatter

In one famous style of abstract art, the artist splatters paint onto a canvas using paintbrushes and other tools.

Texture

Abstract art can also use textures such as cracked or peeling paint as part of the painting itself.

Art Camp

Celebrate your friends and family by holding an art camp where everyone can come together to create artwork. Then put on a show that displays their creations.

You Need

- Paper
- Drawing tools (markers, pencils, crayons, etc.)
- Tape
- Decorations (optional)
- Other art supplies (optional)
- Old newspapers
- Awards

1. Draw up some invitations for your guests. Let them know the time and place of your art camp.

2. Decorate your art camp space however you like. Make sure there are enough art supplies for everyone to share and enough space for each artist to draw or paint. If you like, you can cover a table with newspaper to help keep things clean.

3. When everyone arrives, have your campers start making art. If you want, you can provide some fun ideas or prompts for them, or let them use their imaginations.

4. At the end of camp, host an art show where everyone can show off their art. Have everyone who wants to present their masterpiece. When you are ready, give an award to each piece, with titles like "Most Inspiring," "Most Adorable," "Most Colorful," and more.

Use this space to draft your masterpiece for your art camp.

Ask a parent or guardian if you can draw on an old piece of clothing with fabric markers.

Quick Challenges
EXPRESS YOURSELF

What do you think you look like when you are happy? What about when you are angry, excited, or scared? Draw some of your expressions here.

Draw a personal design for yourself here. It could be something that represents you, something you would wear on your clothes, or something else.

Design a cartoon version of yourself.

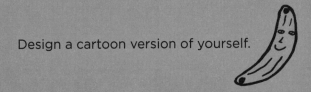

Draw a hand like this one. How many different drawings can you create from it?

Make a drawing inspired by one of your dreams.

Self-Portrait

Draw your self-portrait using a mirror. A self-portrait is a picture an artist makes of themself.

Tip!
Try using a phone or camera to take a picture of yourself. This way you won't be moving while you are trying to draw yourself!

Draw a few more self-portraits from memory.
What differences do you see?

Map It Out

Pick a place like your room, your home, or your neighborhood (or all three), and draw a map of it on the next page. What secret spots will you include? Use symbols to represent different spots on your map that someone could find or visit. Make sure to include a legend!

Map Symbols

A map legend, or map key, explains the symbols you use on your map. For example, if you use a symbol shaped like a triangle to represent trees, people could find out what the triangles meant by looking at the legend. Legends can also tell people how to measure distances on maps, how high or low the land is, and more. People have been using legends for more than 2,500 years.

Legend

Hidden Pictures

There are 20 of the same object hidden in this scene. What is the object? Can you find them all?

Draw your favorite place to play, or design a supercool playground you'd love to visit.

Pet Portrait

Draw a portrait of your pet . . . or of a pet you wish you had!

Now design a fancy home or bed for your pet to relax in.

Critter Comic

Imagine your favorite animal as a superhero. Design your animal character below and draw their adventures on the opposite page.

Hero Card

Describe your animal hero here:

Species: _____

Superhero Name: _____

_____

Superpowers: _____

_____

Make Your Own Cards

Make a card for a friend or family member who could use some cheering up.

Simple Card

You Need

- Paper
- Scissors (optional)
- Markers or colored pencils

1. Fold a piece of paper in half. If you want, use scissors to cut your card into a fun shape like a heart.

2. Draw a picture on the front of your card that you think will make the person smile.

3. Draw some more images on the inside or write something nice. You can tell them that you are thinking of them or let them know you care about them.

4. Give them your card!

Tip!
Have an adult help you find a program that lets you send cards to nursing homes, and draw someone a nice card.

Pop-Up Card

1. Fold two pieces of paper in half from top to bottom. One will be the outside of the card. The other will be the inside of the card.

2. To make the pop-up part, cut an even number of slits in the middle of the folded edge of the inside piece. These should be at least an inch long.

3. Open the folded paper with the slits, and then pull the crease forward for the section you just cut, and re-crease it so it pops forward instead of backward.

4. Glue the edges of the outside card to the inside card. Be sure not to put glue where the folded sections pop out.

5. On the third piece of construction paper, draw an image that you want to pop out. This can be a flower, an animal, a cool robot, or anything else. It should be smaller than the size of your card when it is folded.

6. Cut out your drawing. Glue it to one side of a popped crease so that it pops up when you open the card.

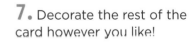

7. Decorate the rest of the card however you like!

Fantastic Feast

Draw a feast of your favorite foods.

Design the ultimate cake for dessert! How many layers does it have? What flavors? Is it actually made of cake, or is it made of something else, like ice cream?

Create a Crest

A crest or a coat of arms often includes things that represent you. Use the space below to doodle items that you might want to include. Try your pets, favorite foods, favorite colors, and other things that are important in your life. Then pick out some (or all) of your drawings to put together on the next page to make a coat of arms for you, your family, or you and a friend.

Cool Crests

A coat of arms (sometimes called a family crest) was a decoration worn by medieval European knights to represent their families. Knights wore these coats of arms on their shields and sometimes on their clothing. Many coats of arms looked like a shield divided into four sections and included animals, symbols, and objects that represented the family. Some coats of arms also had animals on either side of the shield, a helmet above it, and a family saying, known as a motto, below the shield.

Channel Your Feelings

Art is a great way to help express your emotions, whether you're feeling angry, sad, worried, or confused. The next time you feel one of these things (or any emotion that you'd like to express), try creating abstract drawings here and on the next page that represent how you feel.

Pick a favorite book or movie, and then draw yourself as a character in it.

Quick Challenges
ADVENTURE

Pretend you are an explorer. What gear would you need? Design some cool gadgets.

Draw and cut out superhero masks for yourself and your friends.

Draw a comic with your friends. One friend draws the first panel, another friend draws the next, and so on. See how your surprise adventure turns out.

 Pretend you are a spy. Send a coded message to a friend using only pictures.

Turn a paper bag into a cool costume helmet. Cut out a hole for your face and decorate the rest. It could look like the helmet for an astronaut, a knight, a scuba diver, or something else!

Out of This World

Blast off! You are traveling to the far reaches of outer space.
Draw a rocket like the one here or draw one from your imagination.

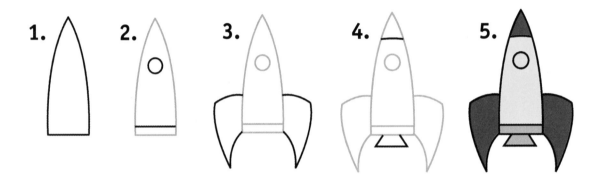

You encounter another spaceship! What does it look like? Who is in it? What kind of cool technology does it have?

Tic Tac Row

Each of these aliens has something in common with the other two aliens in the same row. For example, in the top row across, all three aliens have a UFO behind them. Can you tell what's alike in each row—across, down, and diagonally?

You've landed on an uncharted planet . . . and come face-to-face with an alien civilization! Draw the aliens here. Are they friendly? Do they have any alien pets?

Explore an Ancient Tomb

You've discovered a lost city! What amazing things do you find?
Color in the picture below and then draw your own on the next page.

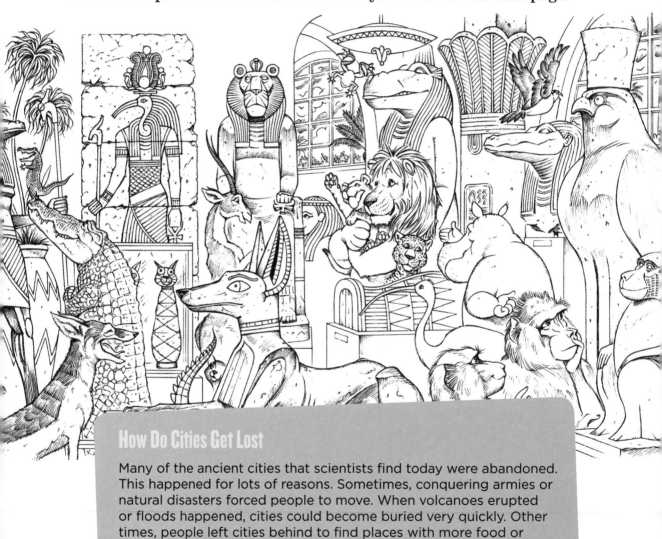

How Do Cities Get Lost

Many of the ancient cities that scientists find today were abandoned.
This happened for lots of reasons. Sometimes, conquering armies or
natural disasters forced people to move. When volcanoes erupted
or floods happened, cities could become buried very quickly. Other
times, people left cities behind to find places with more food or
better access to trade. With everyone gone, the cities would slowly
start to crumble . . . and be swallowed back up by nature.

Optical Illusions

Things aren't always as they seem! Use the instructions below to create some magic for your eyes.

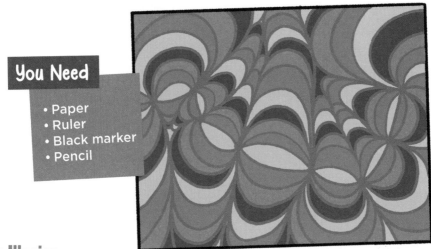

You Need

- Paper
- Ruler
- Black marker
- Pencil

Line Illusion

1. Using the ruler, draw three parallel lines of the same length.

2. Turn the top line into an arrow by adding fins to one end of the line and an arrow point to the other end of the line like this >——>.

3. Add fins to each end of the middle line like this >——<.

4. On the bottom line, add arrow points to both ends of the line like this <——>.

5. Test out your optical illusion. The lines are all the same length . . . but do they look it?

Jagged Lines

1. Using a ruler, draw three to five thin parallel lines at a diagonal angle.

2. On every other line, draw short, thick vertical lines running through it.

3. Draw short, thick horizontal lines running through the remaining lines.

4. Test out your optical illusion. Ask a friend or family member whether the thin lines are parallel to each other.

Try coming up with your own optical illusion. Can you make a drawing that looks like magic?

Deep-Sea Dive

These scuba divers are exploring the sea.
What surprising sight is waiting for them?
Could it be a giant sea creature? A mermaid
tea party? Or something else?

Starring...You!

Make a comic of an adventure you've had with someone important to you. Did you go camping with a relative? Build a fort with a friend? Try new foods with a sibling? Draw it here. Then make a second version (or a copy) and send it to the person who shared your adventure. Make sure to tell them why it was special to you.

1.

2.

3.

4.

5.

6.

7.

8.

9.

10.

Treasure Hunt

Can you find a path to the buried treasure? Start at the 5 in the top left corner. You may move to a new box by adding 5 or subtracting 3. Move up, down, left, or right.

START

5	10	17	10	7	12
5	7	12	13	4	9
11	6	9	8	21	18
16	19	6	11	16	15
13	18	20	12	21	12
10	15	17	15	20	17

FINISH

You've found the treasure! What's inside?

Buried Treasure

Did pirates really bury treasure? As it turns out, not many pirates actually hid their treasure by burying it—it would have been too easy for other people to find. Most treasure was split up among the crew. But some pirates did bury their loot! One such pirate was the infamous Captain William Kidd, who buried his treasure on an island off New York.

Once Upon a Time

Discover the magic of drawing a unicorn with this guide.

1.

2.

3.

4.

Fill this magical land with unicorns, dragons, fairies, and anything else you can dream up.

Make Chores Fun

Draw and decorate a chore chart that turns your weekly chores into awesome adventures.

You Need

- Ruler
- A large piece of paper
- Markers or colored pencils
- A frame with a glass front (optional)
- A dry-erase marker

1. Using your ruler, draw a grid on your paper that shows the days of the week like the one pictured below. Write the days of the week at the top of the grid.

2. On the left side of the grid, list your chores . . . but turn them into imaginary adventures!

3. Decorate your chart with drawings of your adventures, or however else you like.

4. Have an adult help you place your chart in a frame with a glass front. (If you don't have a frame, just tape the paper somewhere in your house!)

5. Each day, check off your adventures using your dry-erase marker.

Chores Checklist

Day/Adventure	Mon	Tues	Wed	Thurs	Fri	Sat	Sun
Explore a lost city (Clean my room)	😀						
Have an octopus tea party (Do the dishes)		😀					
Tame a lion (Walk the dog)							
Study magic (Do my homework)							

Brainstorm ideas for your own unique chore chart here.

6

Quick Challenges
BLAST FROM THE PAST

Draw what you think your parents, grandparents, or guardian looked like when they were kids.

Look up ancient Egyptian hieroglyphs, and then draw your name.

Draw your favorite meal from the past week.

Draw the first memory you can recall.

 Find a drawing that you made when you were younger. Try drawing the same thing again and see how much you've improved!

Some of the first-ever drawings were made using shapes and patterns. Try making a drawing with just patterns.

Doodle, Partner!

Howdy, Sheriff, and welcome
to the Wild West. Design
your badge here.

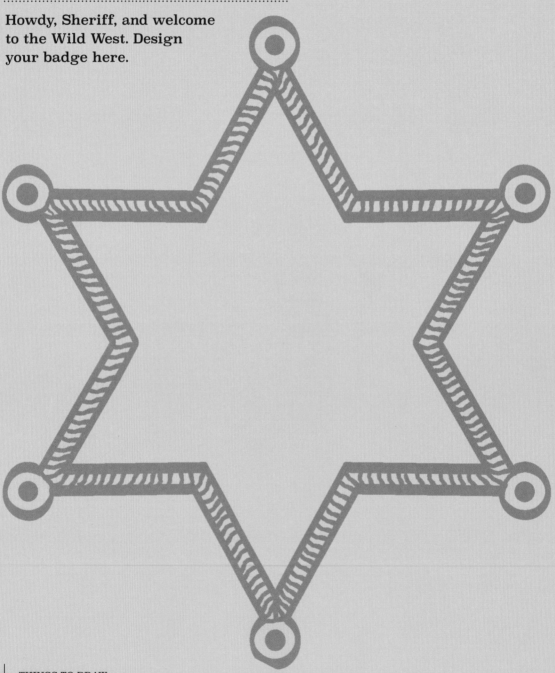

Whoa, there! What are you wranglin'?

Hidden Pictures

The king is throwing a festive party! Can you find all the objects hidden in this image?

ladder

canoe

drinking straw

ring

paper airplane

egg

leaf

book

snow cone

tweezers

lollipop

kite

crescent moon

snail

boot

pennant

elf's hat

boomerang

mug

snake

fishhook

Design a grand castle where all
these merrymakers can celebrate!

Medieval Manuscripts

Design an "illuminated" version of the first letter of your name.

1. Lightly draw the first letter of your name with the pencil.

2. Using the colored pencils or markers, draw a new outline around the basic letter you made in step 1. Leave some space between your new outlines and the original letter.

3. Erase the original letter and any other lines you want gone.

4. Add some embellishments to the outline. These can be swirls, fun shapes, animals, or whatever else you can think of.

5. Decorate your letter with patterns and more images, and then color it in.

Awesome Illumination

In medieval Europe, books were written by hand and were a lot rarer than they are today. Artists took special care to illustrate these books, creating what are known as illuminated manuscripts. Illuminated manuscripts were often decorated with gold and silver. Many times, the artists decorated the letters themselves with fancy designs and/or drawings of people, places, and animals.

Try to hand-letter the whole alphabet or your name, with each letter expressing a different feeling.

Shadow Art

Shadow art has been a form of entertainment for hundreds of years. Make your own with these steps.

You Need

- Sturdy construction paper or cardstock
- Markers or pencils
- Scissors
- Glue or tape
- Recycled straws or craft sticks
- A dark room
- A wall
- Flashlight

1. Draw some large outlines, or silhouettes, of images on your paper. These are easiest when they're simple like the ones here, but try experimenting however you want.

2. Use scissors to cut out your silhouettes.

3. Using glue or tape, attach the images to recycled straws or craft sticks.

4. Turn out the lights in a room where you have space on an empty wall. Shine the flashlight at one of your silhouettes so that its shadow appears on the wall.

5. If you want, act out a story using your shadow art.

Draw some sketches here to get started.

Draw Your Memories

What are some of the best memories you have? Draw some memories here.

What are some new memories you would like to make?

Cave Art

Try drawing some patterns based on your hand, an animal, or something from your imagination. Then on the next page, decorate the cave with your art and patterns.

Cave Art

Humans have been making art for a very long time. In fact, the oldest art ever discovered is more than 43,000 years old! This earliest form of art is known as cave art. People used red and black colors made from clay and plants to draw animals, people, shapes, and more. People often added the outlines of their hands—possibly to communicate with others or to sign their art.

Draw Dinosaurs

Fill this prehistoric land with your favorite dinosaurs. To get started, try drawing these dinos and adding them to the scene.

1.　**2.**　**3.**

4.　**5.**

1.　**2.**　**3.**

4.　**5.**

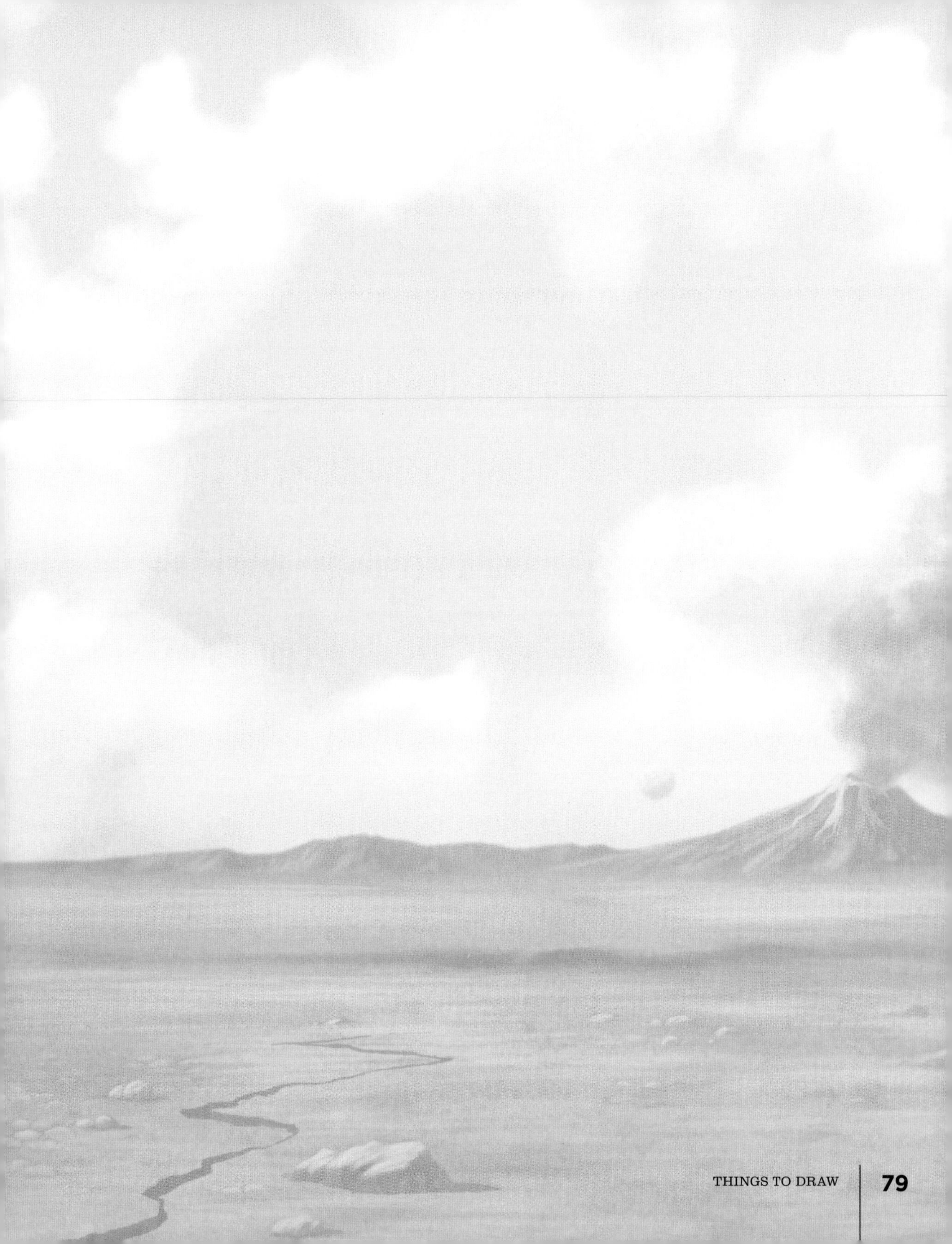

Picture the Past

Draw a picture of your past self here. What was different about you? How have you changed?

Is there anyone or anything from your past that you miss?
Perhaps an old friend, a family member, or a stuffed animal?
Draw them here.

More Ideas! Make a card for the person, animal, or item you miss. It's okay if you can't send it to them—it can feel good just to draw it!

Trace the shadows of leaves here. You can do this by sitting under a tree that is casting a shadow or by holding a fallen leaf over the page so it casts a shadow.

Quick Challenges NATURE

Place a leaf underneath a piece of paper. Lightly rub a pencil or a piece of charcoal over the part of the paper where the leaf is to make a leaf rubbing.

Draw a design here, and then recreate it as temporary art in sand or dirt.

Draw a still life of fruit, vegetables, flowers, or other plants.

 Design as many snowflakes as you can here—remember to make each one different!

Try different ways to capture the colors of a sunset: pastel pencils, crayons, watercolors, and more.

Draw the Seasons

Decorate this tree to show how it would look during the four seasons. What animals would you see here during each season?

Spring

Summer

Fall

Winter

Campsite Sighting

Sometimes it's great to get lost in nature. Follow the line and find your way out of this maze, and then re-create a life-size version outside using chalk.

START

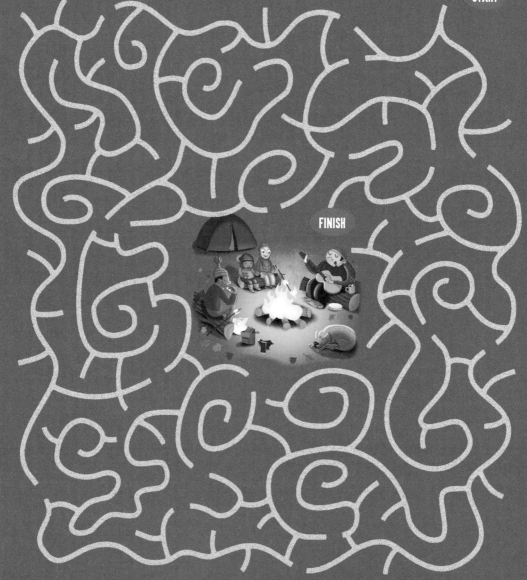

FINISH

Sketch your life-size maze here.

Draw the Stars

With an adult, go outside on a nice night and look at the stars. Draw the stars you see here. Do the stars look the same the next night? Look up the constellations that are visible in your area. Can you see any?

Design a new constellation here.

Star Pattern

A constellation is a group of stars that forms a pattern in the sky. Humans have been seeing images in the stars for thousands of years and giving these patterns names. Today, astronomers recognize 88 constellations that can be seen all over the world. Some can only be seen in certain parts of the world at certain times. More than half of these constellations were named by the ancient Greek people who originally imagined them as images.

In the Pond

Take a swim! What animals have come to visit? On the next page, add some frogs like the one here or draw some other animals and plants from your imagination.

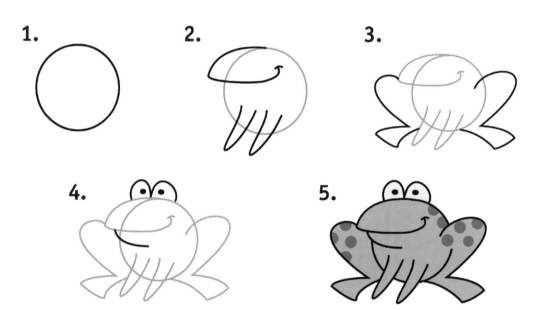

1.

2.

3.

4.

5.

Planet-Saving Poster

Design a poster to encourage others to take care of Earth. What is your message? Will you encourage people to recycle, pick up trash, or something else? What images should you use? Try drafting your message here and designing your poster on the next page.

Tip!
Draw a large version of your poster on poster board or reused cardboard, and hang it where people can see it!

Beautiful Bugs

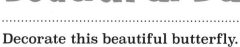

Decorate this beautiful butterfly.

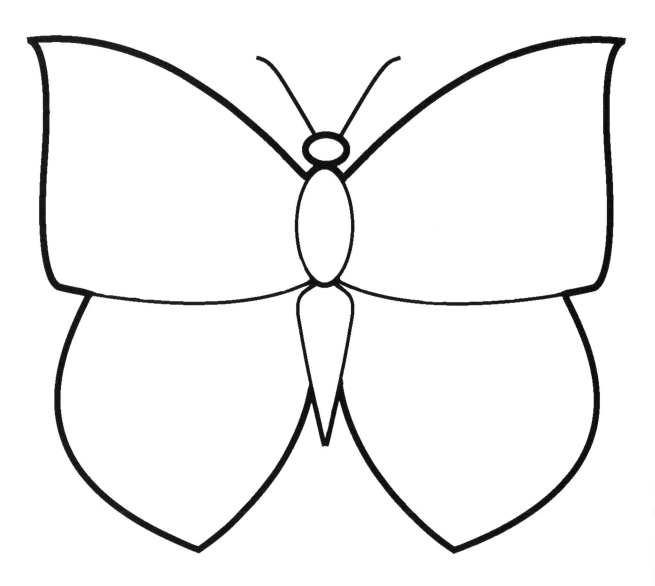

Bzzzz! You've discovered a never-before-seen insect! What does it look like? How big is it? Does it have wings or antennae?

Animal Tracks

What animal tracks can you find in your neighborhood or at your local park? Record them here. Have an adult help you search through some books or online, and then see whether you can figure out what animal made the tracks.

Pawprints

The footprints and pawprints that animals leave behind are known as animal tracks. To identify which animals left the tracks, scientists look at several elements: the number of toes a print has, the size of the tracks, whether the track has nails, the spacing between the tracks, and more.

Window Watching

What's your favorite view? Draw it here in four different kinds of weather. What type of weather is your favorite?

Draw what it would look like if it rained frogs, candy, or something else from your imagination!

Great Gardens

Can you find all the hidden images in the veggie-filled scene below? Then, design your ultimate eco-friendly garden on the next page. What delicious foods would you grow? How would your garden be good for the environment?

fishhook

teddy bear's head

pennant

needle

candle

feather

screwdriver

slice of pie

worm

tack

nail

heart

crescent moon

mushroom

sailboat

magnifying glass

flower

musical note

flag

snow cone

flashlight

mallet

More ideas!
Research what kinds of plants help attract bees and other pollinators. Ask an adult to help you plant some of these in your garden or in a community garden.

Come up with a festive design here, and then decorate a wooden picture frame by drawing or painting the design in a pattern. Give the frame as a gift with a special photo inside.

Draw some wrapped presents here. Then draw on newspaper or large sheets of blank paper to create your own wrapping paper.

Sketch a holiday greeting here. Then draw handmade holiday cards for your friends and family.

Draw some beautiful holiday decorations here. Take it further by making some decorations to hang up during your favorite holiday.

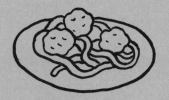

Draw your favorite holiday meal (or candy!) here. Then make dinnertime more festive by drawing name cards for everyone.

Draw a list of gifts you want to give here. Take it further by decorating the cover of a blank journal with your drawings, and then give the journal as a gift.

Make a Monster

These monsters are having a Halloween party!
Create some brand-new monsters here.

Draw the monsters at the party. What is it like?
What will they eat?

Wintery Search

Find all the wintery words in this festive word search.

```
S  H  F  C  A  N  D  L  E  S  A
D  U  V  E  O  A  H  R  A  D  S
N  P  P  Y  C  H  Y  E  S  R  T
E  Y  L  L  O  J  L  E  H  A  F
I  O  S  L  C  I  I  H  A  C  I
R  D  A  N  T  K  M  C  R  Y  G
F  S  G  N  O  S  A  L  E  S  Y
Y  O  J  O  H  W  F  E  O  Z  A
V  A  C  A  T  I  O  N  O  V  S
O  N  E  T  A  R  O  C  E  D  E
G  A  T  H  E  R  E  T  N  I  W
```

WORD LIST

CANDLES	DECORATE	GIFTS	SHARE
CARDS	FAMILY	HOT COCOA	SNOW
CHEER	FRIENDS	JOLLY	SONGS
COOKIES	FUN	JOY	VACATION
COZY	GATHER	LOVE	WINTER

Draw a scene that includes as many of the items found in the puzzle as possible.

Zoo Birthday

How do you think animals at
the zoo celebrate their birthdays?
What kind of gifts would they
want to receive? Draw them here.

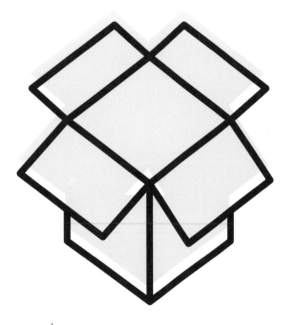

More Ideas!
See if any animal shelters near you take donations like blankets, canned food, or toys. Ask an adult if you can donate something in honor of an animal's birthday.

Birthday Bash

Surprise a friend or family member by drawing birthday decorations for them!

Bunting

You Need

- Paper
- Markers or colored pencils
- Scissors
- String or ribbon
- Tape

1. Draw several large triangles all the same size on the paper.

2. Use the markers to decorate each triangle however you want. Cut out the triangles.

3. Place each triangle in a line with the decorated side facedown and the shortest side at the top.

4. Lay a string or ribbon so that it runs over the short sides of all the triangles.

5. Fold the edge of each triangle over the string, and then secure it in place with tape.

6. Hang your bunting.

Birthday Sign

You Need

- Paper
- Markers or colored pencils
- Scissors (optional)

1. Use your hand-lettering skills (see page 70) to write out the words "Happy Birthday."

2. Decorate them to be as fancy or as colorful as you want.

3. Hang up the sign as a poster or use scissors to cut out each letter and hang those.

Colorful Tablecloth

You Need

- An old tablecloth or sheet
- Markers or colored pencils

1. Have an adult help you find an old tablecloth or an old, clean sheet that you can color on.

2. Use markers to draw all the things the birthday person loves on the cloth.

3. Spread out your tablecloth.

Draw the best gift you have ever gotten—or given—here.
What made it special?

Happy Holidays

What are your favorite holiday traditions?
Draw some here.

Dream up a brand-new holiday tradition and draw it here.

Invent a Holiday

How would you celebrate these holidays? Draw some ideas here.

If you could invent a new holiday for something you love—like a person, a sport, an animal, a favorite toy, or anything else—what would it be? Draw how you would celebrate.

Share Your Art

Art itself can make a wonderful gift for people you care about. Make others smile by creating unique presents for them! These can be for any occasion: holidays, birthdays, special events, or just because. Try out the ideas below, or come up with your own.

Animal Portrait

Draw a portrait of the person's pet, or of their favorite animal.

Abstract Art

Create an abstract masterpiece using the recipient's favorite colors.

Photo Art

Do you have a favorite photograph of you and someone you care about? Create an illustrated version of the picture and give it as a gift.

Comic

Create a comic starring your friend or loved one.

After you've given your art as a gift, draw the recipient's reaction here.

Look at photos of animals with cool patterns, and try drawing their spots and stripes yourself.

Draw some circles here. Can you turn each circle into a different wild animal? See if you can make circles into fish, birds, snakes, or whatever you can think of.

Try to draw an animal out of the letters in its name.

Animals come in all different sizes. What do you think the world looks like to a mouse? Or to a giraffe? Draw a scene from an animal's perspective.

Is there an animal you think is scary? Try drawing a really cute version of it!

Draw a report card for your pet, or for a pet you'd like to have. What are they really good at?

Animal Talk

If animals could talk to people, what would they say? Draw some animals having a conversation and write— or draw—what they are talking about.

Listen to some of the animals around you, like birds, squirrels, dogs, or even bugs, and draw what you think they are talking about.

Doggy Dreams

This pooch is having a sweet dream! Can you find all the hidden objects in this image?

feather **cherry** **bread** **peach** **penny** **peanut** **seed**

What else could this dog be dreaming about? A giant steak?
Flying to the moon in a bone-shaped rocket? Draw it here.

Wild Side

Do you ever dream about being an
animal? What kind of animal would
you be? Draw your new self here.

What would you do? And where would you go? Draw yourself on an epic animal adventure.

Savanna Adventure

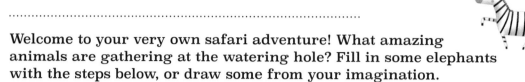

Welcome to your very own safari adventure! What amazing
animals are gathering at the watering hole? Fill in some elephants
with the steps below, or draw some from your imagination.

1.

2.

3.

Amazing Savannas

The African savannas are warm grasslands located mostly in eastern and southern Africa. Small trees dot the landscape here and there, offering shade for animals like lions, cheetahs, and hyenas. Other animals, such as zebras, elephants, and antelopes, move in herds across the grasslands. Because savannas are home to so many kinds of animals, including those that are endangered and threatened, it is important to conserve and protect these lands.

Animal Homes

Just like humans, animals in the wild have all types of homes.
Some, like meerkats, even live underground. Design a cozy
underground den for these marvelous meerkats.

Design an underwater home for this dolphin. Does it decorate with sea stars? Or maybe it stocks its kitchen with sardines? Draw it here.

Animal Rescue

All around the world there are many animals that are endangered or threatened. Luckily, there are lots of ways you can help these animals. Choose an endangered animal and do some reading about it. Sketch a design for a poster that raises awareness about the animal you chose.

Things to Include

1. A drawing of the animal.

2. Information on why the animal needs help. Is its home in danger? Do people hunt the animal? Or is there another reason?

3. List ways that people can help.

Make a final poster with your design, and hang it somewhere people can see it!

Animal Mash-Up

What would an animal with the tail of a pig, the nose of an anteater, the wings of a bird, and the body of an armadillo look like?
Draw it here.

Now draw your own mash-up from three different animals of your choosing.

Rainforest Adventure

Get ready to swing through the trees! Try drawing some monkeys like this one, or draw some from your imagination.

Create a rainforest scene with the animals that call it home.

All About Rainforests

Rainforests are forested habitats that get lots and lots of rain. Scientists split these rainforests into four layers: the uppermost emergent layer, where the tops of the trees are; the canopy, made up of the leaves and branches of the trees; the understory, where smaller trees and plants grow; and the dark forest floor on the ground.

Penguin Pool Party

Splash! It's a penguin pool party! Draw a snowy scene and add some penguins like the one here—or draw some from your imagination.

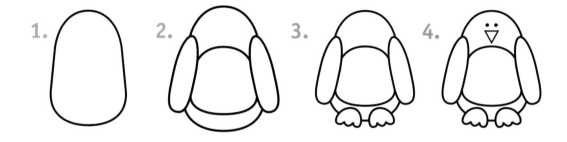

How do you think these penguins warm up after a chilly day?
Draw it!

Prevent Plastic Pollution

Plastic can damage animals' homes, pollute the seas, and harm animals that eat it. Research and draw a list of things people can do to avoid using plastic.

More Ideas!

Have an adult help you organize a local cleanup. This can be at the beach, a local park, a hiking trail, or anywhere else you can pick up litter.

Research

Different places have different rules, so make sure to research the best way to hold a cleanup in your local community. Find out the best gear to keep everyone safe, such as gloves, trash bags, and more.

Draw

To let people know about your cleanup, draw some posters that you can hang around town or get an adult's help to share online. Or draw some invitations for friends and family.

Rules

Make sure to share what you learned about safety and local rules with everyone else.

Draw a quick doodle here. Then try drawing it on unusual materials—like recycled tinfoil—to find cool new effects.

Quick Challenges
THE FUTURE

6

If you are able, visit some art shows or galleries with an adult. Then draw something here using the styles you saw at the shows.

Draw a goal that is important to you. Think about things you can do to achieve this goal. Take it further by drawing your goal on a separate piece of paper and hanging the picture somewhere you can see it.

What do you think you might look like in the future? Draw a portrait.

 Make a time capsule for your future self. Fill it with drawings, photographs, and letters. Put it somewhere safe and open it in the future. Draw yourself a reminder of the time capsule here.

Can you paint something no one has ever painted before? Or can you draw in a brand-new style? Experiment here and find out!

Future Jobs

Would you like to be a famous scientist when you grow up? A trapeze artist? Or how about a rock star? Draw some cool jobs you'd like to try here.

Tip!
Can you think of a new type of job people might do in the future? Perhaps someone might be an alien ambassador or a babysitter for robots? Draw it!

Plan a Dream Vacation

It's time to hit the beach! There are 20 of the same object hidden in this picture. Can you find them all?

Draw what you would pack for your dream vacation.

Future Fun

Uh-oh, while working in the laboratory, you accidentally shrank yourself! Draw the world from your new perspective. What adventures do you have?

What would you do if you had a gadget that could make you invisible? Draw it here.

Design a Futuristic City

What do you think cities of the future will look like? Who would live there? Where would the city be—here on Earth, or somewhere else?

See the Future

Whether or not people can really tell fortunes, imagining the future can be lots of fun! What future do you see in this crystal ball?

Some people use cards to tell fortunes.
What future do your cards hold?

Look Ahead

Do you believe it's possible to
see the future? For thousands
of years, many people have
tried. In ancient Rome, people
believed they could predict
the future based on how birds
behaved and the patterns in
which they flew. This was one
form of an ancient practice
called augury.

Make a Machine

Imagine you are building a machine that can do anything. What does it look like? What does it do? Does it make endless candy? Does it do all your chores? Draw it here.

What are some of your favorite inventions? The computer? The paper clip? How could you improve on these?

Design a Robot

If you could build a robot, what would it look like? What would it do? Try drawing this one here or design one from your imagination on the next page.

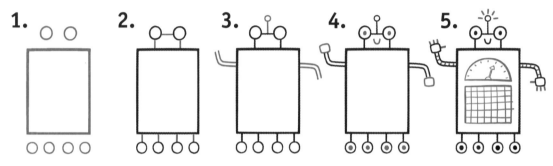

1.

2.

3.

4.

5.

Robots Today

Forget the future—amazing robots are everywhere right now! Scientists have made creations that seem straight out of science fiction. Some are tiny, like nanobots. They can keep a person healthy from inside their body. Some robots, like camera drones or robots with wings, can fly. And there are even robots designed to be good friends for people!

Future Travel

What do you think transportation will look like in the future? Try drawing the truck or boat below, or draw a vehicle from your imagination. Then design some ways people might get from here to there in the future on the next page.

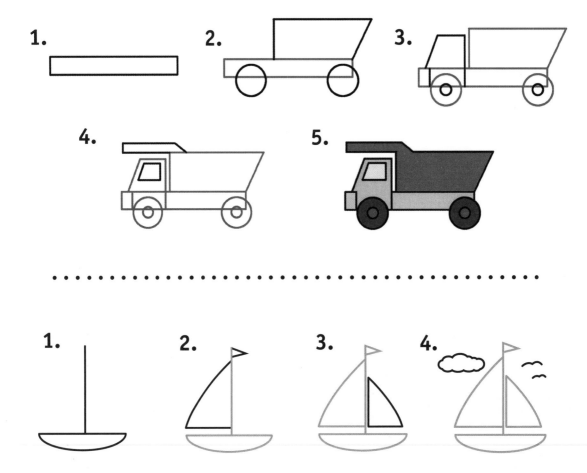

1.

2.

3.

4.

5.

1.

2.

3.

4.

ANSWER KEY

CONNECT THE DOTS
pg 12

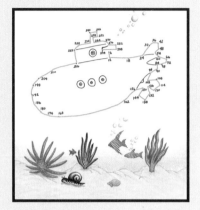

HIDDEN PICTURES
pg 30

TIC TAC ROW
pg 48

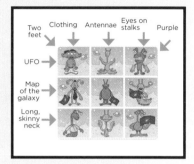

TREASURE HUNT
pg 58

HIDDEN PICTURES
pg 68

CAMPSITE SIGHTING

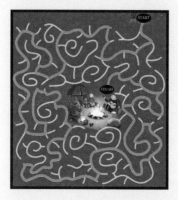

DOGGY DREAMS
pg 122

GREAT GARDENS
pg 100

PLAN A DREAM VACATION
pg 144

WINTERY SEARCH
pg 106

CREDITS

CREDITS

Key: GI=GettyImages, SS=Shutterstock

4: www.facebook.com/okolaamicrostock/GI; 8: MicroStockHub/GI; 14: Andrey Nyunin/SS; 16: klosfoto/GI; 17: Giorez/GI; 18: Juanmoninio/GI (girl, left), LordRunar/GI (girl, right); 19: Antagain/GI (owl), GlobalP/GI (dog and lion); 20: Pobytov/GI; 22: FatCamera/GI; 32: Olga Prokopeva/GI; 34: julos/GI; 38: tenkende/GI; 39: LightFieldStudios/GI; 40: Ricky Saputra/GI; 41: pop_jop/GI; 48: Tamiris6/GI (star background); 51: Givaga/GI; 61: gremlin/GI; 66: ilyast/GI; 67: CSA-Archive/GI; 80-81: boumenjapet/GI (frames), Dimitris66/GI (rainbow background); 82: Iuliia Kanivets/GI (leaves); 83: rambo182/GI (snowflake); 88: AleksandarNakic/GI; 92: Galyna_P/GI; 93: t_kimura/GI; 96: daboost/GI; 98: RADsan/GI; 100: dfli/GI (vegetable garden); 102: bsd555/GI (gift); 103: bortonia/GI (snowman); 106: lilkar/GI; 107: Robert Aneszko/GI; 108: studiostockart/GI (box); 109: Nayanba Jadeja/GI; 110: Retany/GI; 112: filo/GI; 119: bubaone/GI (shark); 120: KenCanning/GI; 123: desifoto/GI (background), SolStock/GI (dog); 128: bucky_za/GI; 131: Artjafara/GI; 136: designer29/GI; 138: Rawpixel/GI; 143: HadelProductions/GI; 145: vectorartnow/GI; 147: designer29/GI; 150: temniy/GI; 151: Natalia Zimicheva/GI

Published by Highlights Press
815 Church Street
Honesdale, Pennsylvania 18431
ISBN: 978-1-64472-782-9
Manufactured in Dongguan, Guangdong, China
Mfg. 07/2021
First edition
Visit our website at Highlights.com.
10 9 8 7 6 5 4 3 2 1
Produced by WonderLab Group, LLC
Writer: Paige Towler
Design: Design Superette, Nicole Lazarus
Copyeditor: Molly Reid
Proofreader: Maya Myers